The
LEADERSHIP SECRETS

of

SANTA
CLAUS™

How To Get Big Things Done
In YOUR "Workshop" …
All Year Long

The  Company

Helping organizations achieve success through Ethical
Leadership and Values-Based Business Practices

To order additional copies of this book, or for information
on other WALK THE TALK® products and services,
contact us at
1.888.822.9255
or visit our website at
www.santassecrets.com

The Leadership Secrets of Santa Claus

Printed in the United States of America
10 9 8 7 6 5

ISBN 1-885228-55-4

Produced by Steve Ventura
Edited by Michelle Sedas
        and Melissa Hazlewood

A SACK FULL OF CONTENTS

Santa's Helpers (The Authors)

Eric Harvey, David Cottrell, Al Lucia, and **Mike Hourigan** have helped hundreds of organizations, and their leaders, build high-performance workplaces – with motivated coworkers.

Their work is based on the belief that effective leaders accomplish "big things" by GIVING employees clear goals, solid accountabilities, and ongoing feedback, coaching, and recognition. These are the leadership traits of the Santa Claus in each of us.

Special thanks to our creative "head elf"

STEVE VENTURA

for helping us get *this* big thing done.

Introduction

It's not easy being Santa Claus!

Believe you me, having to smile and be jolly every day when you're wearing the same thick, hot, red-wool suit (that itches like crazy) is no picnic.

This is a job that will definitely strain your sanity and drain your ego if you let it. Seems like everyone wants a piece of me. Yet many of the people I serve question my existence ... or just plain don't believe in me at all. And those who *do* believe often expect me to do the impossible – rarely caring about what I have to do, or go through (including chimneys), to meet their expectations. And they ALL have expectations.

Give people exactly what they want, and Ho, Ho, Ho – everybody loves good Ol' Santa. But miss one or two items on the list, or forget to include the batteries, and you'd better be ready for the alligator tears, the fat jokes, the stupid songs, no cookies, the wet laps, the yanks on the beard, and the "I could do Santa's job better than Santa" remarks. And that's only half of why it's not easy being me.

There's no doubt that my biggest challenges come from two roles that people rarely associate with this red-cheeked, bag-carrying sleigh driver: Santa the MANAGER and Santa the LEADER.

I am, after all, running a business here. I'm a boss. I've got responsibilities – both to the gift-*getters* and the gift-*makers*. There are workers to lead, letters to read, orders to fill, processes to manage, stuff to buy, stuff to make, standards to maintain, new technologies to adopt, skills to develop, elf problems to solve, and reindeer droppings to scoop (although I delegate that one). Trust me, I've got some big and not-always-easy-fitting boots to fill.

It's true that over the centuries, I've learned a lot from mistakes and miscalculations. One year, for example, my well-planned toy production schedule was thrown completely out of whack by last-minute changes in customer requirements. I thought I had a good read on what the kiddies were wanting, and we had geared up for a big push on dolls and board games. Then a new movie came out and WHAM – all of a sudden everyone now wanted action figures and *video* games. Boy did we do some last-minute scrambling! We were working twenty-four/seven to deal with that one. What a production challenge! What a motivation challenge!

Another year, I had two reindeer come down with the flu right after Prancer pulled the plug, retired, and took off for Florida. That left me with a thirty-three percent delivery staff reduction (if you count Rudolph) with no immediate replacements. And the number of houses to visit had increased by seventeen percent. Talk about "doing more with less"! That year was not only tough on me, but also placed an extra load on the rest of the reindeer. Those puppies were really dragging by the time we finished the last house. We barely made it back. They were ticked and I was tired. But since it takes almost a year to train new harness-team members, there was no rest to be enjoyed. I had to immediately post the open positions and start reviewing reindeer résumés.

Like most managers, I have to deal with marketplace fluctuations ("Dear Santa, I thought I wanted *that*, but now I want *this*."). And I've seen more than my share of budget cuts, staff reductions, employees who are either unwilling or unable to adjust to change, technology advancements, increasing demands for higher quality and better service, fluctuations in the economy, competing priorities, ever-growing performance expectations (for all of us), and a whole lot more. Whew!

Think your job is tough? *You* try recruiting in, and for, the North Pole; *You* try retooling your plant – and retraining your people – every year to produce the newest fads in toys; *You* try delivering tons of presents on a route as big as mine – all in one long night.

No, it's not easy being Santa Claus. But in spite of that, **I love what I do**. People need me ... they depend on me. We're doing something important here. And knowing that gives me the energy to carry the sack, lead the pack, and keep coming back.

By now, you may be wondering how I meet all of these many challenges and responsibilities ... how I manage to bring everyone and everything together to complete our mission. Some people think I use magic. But really, there's no magic about it.

So, if it's not magic, what *is* my secret? Actually there are eight of them – eight practical strategies for leading others and getting big things done all year long. They're called "The Leadership Secrets of Santa Claus," and I'm here to share them *with* you.

They are my gifts *to* you. And I guarantee that if you apply them, you'll find these "secrets" more valuable than anything you might have written on your holiday wish list.

Read on! Lead on!

Santa Claus

1 Build A Wonderful Workshop

MAKE THE MISSION THE MAIN THING

When it comes to getting "big things" done well, there are few (if any) businesses that can hold a Yule candle to our North Pole operation. I'm extremely proud of the workshop that the elves, reindeer, and I have created – and we're more than happy to show it off. But, at ninety degrees North latitude and minus fifty degrees Fahrenheit, we get very few takers on our standing offer to tour the facility. Most Southerners (everyone's a Southerner to us) only see our plant through their imaginations ... through the stereo-typical images they've had of Santa's workshop since childhood.

What's your vision of our workplace? Do you see candy canes and chestnuts? Wood chips flying in the air and falling into neat little piles? Whistling and singing? Busy little elves and reindeer, with smiles on their faces, scurrying around to make and package toys? If so, your image is right on – except for the candy canes and chestnuts ... and the wood chips (we rarely use wood any more).

Yes, we do run a productive and happy place here. And that's in spite of the intense pressures and challenges we face – ones that undoubtedly were *not* included in your vision of us. So how do we do it? Just how do *I* keep everyone, including myself, on track and motivated throughout each long year – all for one long night's big splash? The answer is basic and simple: through an unwavering and uncompromising focus on OUR MISSION. And as the leader,

I've taken several steps to establish and maintain that focus:

First, I've made sure that all the elves and reindeer know what our mission is ("Making spirits bright by building and delivering high-quality toys to good little girls and boys") and why it's important. Ask any member of our North Pole staff and they can quote our mission verbatim ... *and* explain its significance.

Second, I've spent time with individual employees – discussing how their respective jobs specifically link with, and contribute to, the accomplishment of our mission.

Third, I've kept the mission "in front of folks" by posting it on walls, discussing it at staff meetings and training sessions, including it in internal correspondence, and through a host of other activities that help ensure it stays our central focal point.

Finally, I've made it a core component of our decision-making and work-planning processes. If an action we're considering doesn't support our mission, either directly or indirectly, we don't do it!

With all the team members we have, orders we get, toys we make, and issues we face, it could be way too easy to dilute ourselves, head off on tangents, or just plain lose sight of why we're here. We avoid those by keeping our mission at the heart of everything we do ... by making our mission our main thing. I recommend that you do the same in *your* workshop.

FOCUS ON YOUR PEOPLE AS WELL AS YOUR PURPOSE

Here's a nugget of leadership wisdom that I've picked up over the decades – something you can take to one of the toy banks we occasionally deliver: You can't possibly focus on your mission without also focusing on the folks that make your mission happen. The two go hand in hand ... hoof in hoof (sorry, but the reindeer insisted). And besides, since you manage *things* and lead *people*, common sense suggests that it's *people* who are at the core of all leadership activities.

But alas, common sense apparently isn't all that common. There is a handful of managers out there who don't get it – they don't get the message, and they don't get the positive results that the message can help produce. That point was clearly brought home by a short letter I received several years ago:

> *Dear Santa:*
> *This year I only want one thing – a manager who cares as much about me as the work I'm doing. It's hard to be committed when there's no reciprocation. Please help!*

Now that's a sad commentary ... and a tall order to fill. There was no need to check our production schedule. I already knew that "caring leaders" weren't on our list of deliverables. But I needed to respond in some way, so I decided to do two things: 1) Write this book, and 2) Vow to do my very best never to be the kind of leader described in that letter.

I'm happy (even jolly) to say I've done both. Writing this book was by far the easier of the two responses; living up to my vow – turning my good intentions into predictable behaviors – was more challenging. It took abandoning a few old behaviors and adopting a few new ones; it required commitment, self-discipline, concentration, and prioritization. And I needed to monitor my progress (and still do), through both self-evaluation and periodic feedback from the workshop team, by providing answers to the following:

In the last several months, what have I done to ...

- ... Be accessible (physically and mentally) to employees who would like my attention?
- ... Be considerate of staff-member needs?
- ... Provide employees with the training, tools, resources, and feedback required for success?
- ... Keep employees in the "what's happening" information loop?
- ... Help team members maintain an appropriate balance between their professional and personal lives?
- ... Demonstrate respect for employees' time and talents ... as well as respect for them as individuals?
- ... Solicit, and listen to, staff-member ideas and concerns?
- ... Help everyone develop and grow?
- ... Fairly distribute the work and workload?

These, and many others like them, are the questions I ask – and the things I do – to make sure I focus on the wonderful workers who comprise our wonderful workshop. What questions do *you* ask? What action items would I find on *your* list?

LET VALUES BE YOUR GUIDE

Every once in a while, a truly special moment occurs in education – the *student* turns out to be the *teacher*. I experienced one of those moments not too long ago, and I'd like to share it with you. This next leadership lesson comes courtesy of a savvy little elf named Virginia.

It was a Tuesday morning and I was conducting a leadership development training session in the workshop classroom. I gave each participant a set of plastic building blocks along with an assignment: "Build a model of a wonderful workshop." The purpose of the task was twofold: 1) Test student creativity and thinking, and 2) Provide me with ideas for improving our North Pole facility. After starting the exercise, I left the room.

I returned an hour later and found that everyone was busy building his or her structure – everyone, that is, except Virginia. She was just sitting there, staring into space. "Is there a problem, Virginia?" I inquired. "No, Santa," she replied, "I'm just thinking." So I left her to her thoughts and exited the classroom.

After another hour had passed, I returned to the room to conclude the exercise. As I moved from table to table, I was truly impressed by the array of detailed models with structural components like smoke stacks, loading ramps, conveyor belts, sleigh landing pads, cafeterias, gyms, offices, and even high-tech classrooms.

When I came to Virginia's model, however, I was taken aback. There, in front of her, were six vertical columns – and nothing more. "Need more time?" I asked. "No thanks," she answered, "I'm done." Hearing that, I probed further: "Virginia, I'm not sure I understand. All the other models are very detailed structures, but all you have are six columns. No walls, no roof, no nothing. How come?" The explanation she offered is where you'll find the lesson for leaders everywhere:

"Well, Santa, it seems to me that what makes a workshop wonderful is not walls and ceilings, but what happens *inside* those walls and *under* those ceilings ... it's not how a workshop *stands*, but what it *stands for* that makes it special. These six columns you see are pillars, and they represent values – the values of respect, integrity, quality, customer service, responsibility, and teamwork. I found them listed on our website. Maybe for some folks they're just words, but for me, they're blueprints to follow. And that's where leadership comes in. **Making sure that everyone knows what values are important**, and then **helping everyone turn those good beliefs into everyday behaviors** is how leaders create a great place to work. At least that's how I see it. And that's why my model looks the way it does. Did I do okay?"

With a huge grin on my face and a twinkle in my eye, I responded: "Yes, Virginia, that *is* a wonderful workshop. And I think that you are going to be a wonderful leader. Thank you for giving me such a valuable gift."

BUILD A WONDERFUL WORKSHOP

- Make The Mission The Main Thing

- Focus On Your People As Well As Your Purpose

- Let Values Be Your Guide

2 Choose Your Reindeer Wisely

HIRE TOUGH SO YOU CAN MANAGE EASY

You know Dasher and Dancer, Prancer and Vixen; Comet and Cupid, Donner and Blitzen. But do you recall the *least* famous reindeer of all: Misfit? Probably not. He's not here anymore. Unfortunately, I had to let him go decades ago. But I certainly learned a lot from the whole Misfit experience.

It all started when I was faced with hiring a new reindeer to fill a vacant position. Now, I know that pulling the sleigh is a very important job. Ask the reindeer – they'll tell you. But I was busy – very busy. Recruiting and hiring a new puller was just one of the scores of things on Santa's platter. And besides, bringing on new staff can be tedious, bureaucratic, and tiring work. It's not what makes me jolly. Personally, I'd much rather walk around the workshop, chat with the elves, and test the new toys. So, I took the easy route. I did a cursory résumé review, conducted a quick, pro forma interview, and grabbed the first warm, antlered-body that appeared halfway decent.

Did I probe to determine if Misfit was committed to responsibilities like teamwork, dependability, and customer service? No. Did I test his flying skills? No. Did I do a thorough background check? No. Did I involve any of the other reindeer in the selection process? No. Did I take one of our new, high-pressure water gun toys and shoot myself in the proverbial foot? YES!

Misfit was appropriately named all right. After a short period of putting his best hoof forward, the problems began. He'd show up late, and then display a less than desirable attitude when I called him on it. More and more, he'd carry less and less of his share of the load. That made the sleigh pull to the right – forcing the left side crew to work harder in order for us to stay straight. The harder they worked, the more irritated they became ... and the harder it was for me to keep the reins in check.

I ended up spending way too much time watching Misfit, re-re-re-training him, counseling him, and handling complaints about him from the other reindeer – and the elves as well. Pretty soon, he was bringing the whole team down. And productivity was going down with them. All of that because of one Misfit reindeer ... all of that because I cut corners and allowed joining the team to be way too easy.

That was then. Now I do things much differently. Through the Misfit experience, I've come to realize that:

1. Because it's employees who ultimately make our mission happen, staffing is my single most important responsibility;

2. The time I spend hiring the right way is nothing compared to the time I'll *have* to spend dealing with the wrong reindeer.

Take a hiring lesson from Santa. Invest in doing it right up front and everyone – especially you – will be happier down the road.

PROMOTE THE RIGHT ONES ... FOR THE RIGHT REASONS

Just listen to his cute little song (go ahead ... sing it to yourself) and you'll quickly realize that Rudolph wasn't always the lead reindeer. In fact, he didn't get that promotion until one foggy night about a century ago. Before that, Donner had the top spot; Donner was "the deer." And as it turned out, promoting Donner was "the problem."

Now don't get me wrong, Donner was not a bad reindeer. He was a great reindeer! One of the best pullers I've ever had. He was strong, fast, and dependable; he pulled more than his weight (and he weighed a ton). He followed instructions to the letter. Donner was a pro – as a puller. So when it came time to promote a new lead, he was my obvious choice. He had earned it. And I assumed that the best puller would make the best leader. Well, to quote another old song title, "it ain't necessarily so." And he proved it.

To say that Donner had a difficult time is an understatement. The lead job was different than the puller job – with skill and ability requirements that I hadn't tested for and that he couldn't meet. He was in over his head, and he was miserable. So were the other reindeer ... and so was I. It's no secret that I was a little short on the "Ho, Ho's" during that period. Donner needed to go back to the job he was good at, and a new lead – the right lead – needed to be found.

Lead reindeer ("RD1"on our classification sheet) is an important position. The lead has more contact with the pullers than anyone else here at the Pole ... and a lot more influence over them as well. It was critical that I pick a leader that the other deer would follow. And there stood Rudolph.

Rudolph was a decent puller, but by no means was he the strongest or fastest of the crew. When he first joined the team, some of the other reindeer laughed, called him names, and excluded him from their games. They're not an easy bunch to "bond" with. But that changed as they (and I) began to notice that there was something special about Rudolph; he seemed to have a knack for getting things done with others ... a nose for leadership. So I decided to consider him for the lead.

This time, I grabbed my laptop and started to type some notes. I created two columns: 1) The tasks, duties, and responsibilities of the lead position, and 2) The characteristics, talents, values, abilities, and attitudes that I felt were necessary to perform those tasks successfully – and to support our overall mission. Then I tested Rudolph and the other candidates against those criteria. He was a standout. He had "the right stuff."

So, on that foggy night long ago, Rudolph got his shot. And the rest, as they say, is history. It's a *wonderful* history ... and an unforgettable lesson.

GO FOR THE DIVERSITY ADVANTAGE

Not all of what I've learned about hiring came from reindeer experiences. And since our other group of workers tend to get a little miffed if they don't get equal time, here's Santa's third and final lesson on employee selection – involving the elves:

It used to be that our elves were pretty much all alike – same size, same pointed ears, same little green suits, same way of talking ... same everything. Whenever we needed new elves, I automatically looked for, and brought on, workers that fit the standard mold. Why not? That's the way it was for years and years – and it seemed to be working just fine. We rarely messed up an order and we had never missed our December twenty-fourth delivery. I was one happy sleigh driver – that is, until two things happened.

First, I found out that we had competitors. Department stores, on-line retailers, discount chains, and a whole host of other manufacturers and toy distributors were moving in on the market we had cornered for decades. They had all kinds of workers (not just elves), and they were gaining ground on our operation. To add insult to injury, some of them were actually using phony Santas – imposters dressed up like me ... pretending to be me.

I wasn't sure how to address the challenge of competition, but I knew that *something* needed to be done. Staying with "business as usual" probably wouldn't serve us well that much longer.

Soon after discovering that we had competition, the second thing happened: A group of North Pole politicians (yes, we have them too) passed a law that said we had to expand our hiring practices; we had to start bringing on "different" kinds of toy makers – not just the little pointy-eared fellas we'd been employing forever. So we complied with the regulations and came face-to-face with a *new* set of challenges. We had *not-the-same-old-elves* recruiting procedures to develop and coworker acceptance issues to deal with. Since not everyone spoke Northpolese, there were some language barriers to hurdle. New interpersonal skills had to be developed. And things called "nondiscrimination regulations" had to be communicated, taught, and followed.

It wasn't easy, but we did it. We did it all. And in the process, we got more than a Santa's sack full of unexpected benefits. It didn't take long to discover that our "different" toy makers came bearing gifts. They brought new skills, perspectives, and ideas to the work-shop. They gave us more than one way of thinking, planning, pro-ducing, and problem solving. They made us better, stronger, and much more in touch with the "different" shapes, sizes, and colors of customers that we serve. And all that has helped us more than hold our own with all those competing Santa wannabes out there.

What started out as a challenging situation – to merely comply with a requirement – has become our most significant competitive advantage. And it can be yours as well. Believe Santa Claus ... believe in diversity.

CHOOSE YOUR REINDEER WISELY

- Hire Tough So You Can Manage Easy

- Promote The Right Ones ... For The Right Reasons

- Go For The Diversity Advantage

3 Make A List and Check It Twice

PLAN YOUR WORK

Respond to endless streams of request letters, make millions of high-quality products – according to exact specifications – three hundred and sixty-four days a year, package the toys so they arrive in perfect condition, and deliver the exact right gift to the exact right person in the exact right house millions of times in one single night. Then, immediately begin working on the next season's demands – which inevitably include *more* kids, *more* homes, an *expanded* service area, and *fewer* (and smaller) chimneys. That's what we do every year. We do it flawlessly ... and none of it happens by accident. Our success – and resulting reputation for excellence – is the result of clearly defined goals combined with well-thought-out plans to accomplish those goals.

We begin by breaking down our one huge annual goal (our mission) of "delivering the goods" into a series of manageable, bite-size sub-goals. We have them for the shop in general, the teams within the shop, and individuals within the teams.

Whether in direct production and delivery, or a "behind the scenes" support function, *everyone* has goals – including me. Our goals are specific yet flexible – allowing for changing conditions and circumstances. And because staff "buy-in" and commitment is so important to achieving our objectives, I make sure that *everyone* has input in the goal-setting process.

Once our individual and group goals are identified, the planning (making "the list") phase. Plans provid direction, focus, and organization we need to stay o since none of us here at the Pole have perfect memo sure that they're *written* action plans.

We develop our plans by answering six questions for each set goal:

1. **WHAT** needs to be accomplished?
2. **WHY** does it need to be done? (How does it contribute to our overall mission?)
3. **WHEN** does it need to be accomplished?
4. **WHERE** am I/are we now in relation to this goal?
5. **WHO** will be involved in accomplishing this?
6. **HOW** will it be accomplished? (What specific steps and activities are involved, and what resources are required?)

After answering these questions with as much detail as possible, we perform the last of the planning activities: adding contingencies. We do our best to anticipate the unexpected by asking *But what if ...* questions. *But what if the snowfall is way above or below normal this year? But what if a flu bug works its way through the shop during peak production time? But what if the computer with our delivery address book crashes?* Certainly we can't predict all the obstacles we may face, but combining some thought with past experiences does enhance our readiness to deal with that fellow Murphy's law.

YOUR PLAN

Several years ago, in an effort to meet our growing production demands, we started making "assembly required" toys. We spent a great deal of time and effort developing detailed instruction booklets that even a child could follow. But then, we started to receive lots and lots of e-mails, with attached photos (of final products that looked nothing like our original designs), claiming that our toys were faulty. We investigated. The problem was that the *children* weren't doing the assembly – the *parents* were. And they were ignoring the instructions. The plans we had worked so hard to create were, in many cases, useless. They had become nothing more than an academic exercise because they weren't being followed. The key learning: Ya gotta follow the plans – whether you're assembling toys or working to achieve your goals. We most definitely have put that learning to good use. So should you.

Once a reasonable plan is made, we immediately implement it. Acting quickly is an imperative for our business. Don't get me wrong, we *do* think things through carefully. But we're also careful to avoid the "paralysis of analysis" that often accompanies the pursuit of elusive plan perfection. We get things going fast, and then we make midcourse corrections as necessary. And the way we know how we're doing, as well as what adjustments we need to make, is through continual monitoring and measurement.

None of us here at the workshop are particularly fond of
surprises – especially me. They take the twinkle right ou
eyes. Fact is, we face enough challenges already without
turing any more on our own. So we don't wait until estin
completion dates to see if we've reached our goals. Once we make
our list (plan), we check it twice. Actually, we check it a lot *more*
than twice.

We schedule (as in: set specific times on our calendars) frequent
progress checks as part of the work-planning process. I meet with
teams and individuals – and they meet among themselves, without
me – to measure the status of our goals against predetermined progress "benchmarks." At those meetings, we ask the following:

- Is each goal still valid and doable?
- Are we where we should be in terms of attaining each goal?
- Have any conditions or circumstances changed since we
  originally set each goal?
- Do we need to make any changes to our goals, our action
  plans, or our performance levels?

The answers to these questions provide the intelligence we need to
guide us in bringing our important mission to life.

As the sign on our workshop wall says:

**IF WE WANT TO HEAR JINGLE BELLS RINGING ON THE 24TH,
WE NEED TO SET AND LIVE BY GOALS ... ALL YEAR LONG!**

ᴧE THE MOST OF WHAT YOU HAVE

There's another sign hanging in our workshop. It reads
SO MANY TOYS, SO LITTLE TIME
and it serves as a reminder for us (and a clue for you) about over-
coming big challenges and accomplishing big goals: You have to
maximize the resources available to you.

Goal setting – planning your work and then working your plan –
not only leads to effectiveness, it also fosters efficiency ... it helps
you minimize waste. And if there's one thing we hate around here,
it's waste. Considering the volume of orders and deliveries we deal
with annually, we'd quickly go out of business if we didn't make
the absolute best use of our resources: time, money, materials, and
the talents of our elves and reindeer. I can picture the headlines
now: SANTA WASTES AWAY TO NOTHING! (And they would
not be talking about my belly that shakes like a bowl full of jelly!)

Because resources are so important to us, we've gone well beyond
merely relying on goal action plans to ensure efficiency. The best
example of this is a workshop-wide team we created called "Waste
Watchers" (again, no connection with my girth). The sole purpose
of the group is to identify and eliminate inefficient/wasteful business practices. The following page presents just a few of the strategies they've come up with to help us do more with less. I offer it
as yet another gift to you.

Making The Most of TIME

- ✔ Prioritize tasks (do the most important things first) and use "to do" lists to organize daily activities.

- ✔ Start and end meetings promptly – and issue agendas in advance.

- ✔ Teach time-management skills and techniques.

- ✔ Take advantage of timesaving technology.

Making The Most of MONEY

- ✔ Buy in discounted bulk whenever appropriate.

- ✔ Shop for the best prices on materials, supplies, equipment, and services.

- ✔ Use e-mail to reduce postage and long-distance charges.

- ✔ Think pennies as well as dollars – a few cents saved here and there add up quickly.

Making The Most of MATERIALS and EQUIPMENT

- ✔ "Measure twice, cut once."

- ✔ Reuse and recycle whenever possible.

- ✔ Be religious about preventative maintenance.

- ✔ Invest in extended warranties.

Making The Most of EMPLOYEE TALENT and EXPERTISE

- ✔ Involve the *people* with the *knowledge* in the *decisions*.

- ✔ Match jobs with worker skills and interests.

- ✔ Enhance employee expertise through training and developmental assignments.

- ✔ Encourage employees to share their knowledge with others.

MAKE A LIST AND CHECK IT TWICE

- ■ Plan Your Work

- ■ Work Your Plan

- ■ Make The Most Of What You Have

4 Listen To The Elves

OPEN YOUR EARS TO PARTICIPATION

Way, way back when we started in this business, there were a lot less orders to fill and a lot fewer houses to visit. We didn't have even ten percent of the staff we have now, and I did quite a bit of the toy making myself. In fact, I did quite a bit of *everything* myself. But eventually, as our operation grew in size and complexity, it became necessary to move away from "doing" (except for my big deliveries) and devote my time to managing. The good news was that I had a wealth of experience to call upon as a manager. The bad news: I used that experience ... to a fault.

Because I had "been there," I was pretty sure I knew more than – or at least as much as – the elves did about toy production. Don't get me wrong – I was always kind and respectful to my employees. I was quite fond of those little folks in green. Still am. But when a decision needed to be made, it was me alone who made it; when a process needed to be modified or upgraded, I devised the plan; when a color needed to be added, I determined the paint mixture; when new equipment needed to be selected ... oh well, you get the picture. Running the show was my job. Besides, who else could make those calls? Certainly not the elves. They had neither the experience for, nor the interest in, administrative work like that. Or so I thought. Until, that is, one day when out in the workshop there arose such a clatter, I sprang from my office to see what was the matter.

It turns out, the gears of the toy production line had grinded to an unexpected halt. The inspection process that *I* had just implemented (after two weeks of closed-door design) was slowing things to a snail's pace. The elves were going crazy trying to keep up with the production schedule. And then, the new mechanical assembler that *I* researched and purchased let loose with a strange thumping noise, coughed up a billow of smoke, and shut down completely.

A quick investigation revealed that my new procedure and the assembly machine were both flawed. "We could have told you," said one of the elves, "if you just had asked us in the beginning ... and really listened to what we had to say." I responded: "So what can we do to get things going again?" With that, a bunch of them huddled for a little while and came up with a better inspection process – and some modifications that got the assembler up and running again. We were back in business; the elves were patting each other on the back and smiling. And I had come to realize that involving workers in running the operation – and in making decisions that affect them – is a key strategy for leadership success.

Now I ask for (and listen to) the elves' ideas and opinions on most everything we do. I even let *them* make many of the toy-making decisions we face. And the production line has never run better.

PAY ATTENTION TO HOW YOU'RE PERCEIVED

want this ... I want that; Last year's gift was great. This year I'd really like ...; Dear Santa, you are a very nice person. Please bring me ....

That's just a small sampling of the kind of customer feedback I'm constantly receiving here at the North Pole. Do I pay attention to it? You bet your boots (or my boots) I do! It's part of what keeps us in business. Couldn't operate without it. Knowing what people want and need – and especially what they think of us – is critical to our success. And, as mentioned in the previous pages, I've come to realize the importance of listening not only to our customers, but also to our elves, reindeer, and others in Santa's workshop.

As our challenges have grown with each new season, more and more I rely on teamwork, collaboration, and the contributions of each member of the workshop team. Ensuring that those things happen requires effective leadership on my part, and I began to wonder how I was doing on that front. The only way to find out was to ask ... and then listen.

So, I began doing employee attitude surveys and conducting focus groups. I even established a "North Pole feedback hot line" to help find out what everyone thought about me as a leader, and to provide a vehicle for collecting input on how I could improve.

When designing the survey, I went to the professors at NPU (North Pole University) for assistance with question development. I even hired a consultant group to help me organize and interpret the information.

Input forwarded via the employee hot line pinpointed two key requirements necessary for making the process work: 1) I had to constructively accept the feedback I received, and 2) I needed to ACT on the information – to use it as a catalyst for becoming a more effective leader, and for developing a better organization.

Neither of those requirements was particularly easy at first. But it was clear that failing to meet them would hamper my staff's will-ingness to candidly share their feelings and would turn the effort into a meaningless exercise. That would be worse than doing nothing at all.

So I listened ... and I acted. I do to this very day. And I'm a much better Santa because of it. I pay attention to what my elves (and others) feel. Perceptions are realities for those that hold them ... and I must deal with those realities in order to lead effectively. And so, too, must you.

Whether it's through formal surveys, hot lines, informal discus-sions, "slip me an anonymous note about my leadership" invita-tions, or whatever, you must find your own way to ask, listen, and act.

WALK AWHILE IN *THEIR* SHOES

It's true that I'm in the gift-*giving* business. That's what I do ... it's what I live for. But occasionally, I *get* gifts as well. And like everyone else, Santa does have his favorites. My most cherished gift of all occupies a place of prominence on a bookshelf in my office: a pair of green felt elf shoes (the kind with pointed toes that curl up). I received them several years ago. They just appeared on my desk one day, along with a "Dear Santa" letter.

Now this letter was much different than the kind I'm used to reading. It didn't ask for anything. It was a thank you letter. I consider it a written commendation. And with great pride, I offer it as your next leadership lesson:

Dear Santa:

Thank you for being such a great boss. We know it isn't easy being you – with all the pressures and responsibilities that you have. We also know that we're not always the easiest bunch to deal with. But with all that you have going on, and with all that we sometimes throw your way, you still manage to remain considerate and understanding. You show us, by your behaviors, that you realize it's challenging for all of us in the workshop too. That makes us appreciate you even more.

We really do look forward to your regular visits to the shop floor. We like it when you stop to chat with each of us to see how things are going. It hasn't always been that way, but that doesn't matter. It's that way now, and we're grateful that it is.

It's great when you ask us about the problems, challenges, and obstacles that we face in filling our orders and meeting deadlines. You really listen – showing us that our feelings are important ... that we are important.

We like it when you occasionally work next to us – giving us a hand and keeping you in touch with the operation. But the thing we appreciate most is when you ask what you can do to make things easier and better for us, and better for the workshop – and then you DO those that are reasonable and appropriate.

Thank you, Santa, for making the effort to see things through our eyes ... for walking in these smaller, yet none-the-less important shoes. Your feet may not fit in them, but your heart most definitely does.

The Elves

Santa Summary:

LISTEN TO THE ELVES

- Open Your Ears To Participation

- Pay Attention To How You're Perceived

- Walk Awhile In THEIR Shoes

5 Get Beyond The Red Wagons

HELP EVERYONE ACCEPT THE REALITY OF CHANGE

There's an old saying (although it wasn't old when I first heard it ... and neither was I) that goes like this: The only constant in life and in business is CHANGE. And for those of us who live and work at the North Pole, nothing exemplifies that saying more than "red wagons."

It used to be that one of the most popular toys we produced and delivered (thirty-seven percent of our production activities to be exact) were shiny red wagons. Just about every child dreamed of getting one for the holidays. Maybe *you* had one when you were little. If so, there's a good chance it came from us. The elves made tons of them. They loved to make them ... they were good at making them ... they took pride in watching them roll off the assembly line. They were a happy little bunch of "wagon masters" – until the day I had to tell them that, based on the letters I was receiving, the demand for wagons was way down. Video games were "in," and the workshop crew needed to change what they did and how they operated.

I wasn't looking forward to being the messenger on that one. It was going to be a major shake-up that would force the elves out of their comfort zones and throw them into the new and unknown. I knew we had to abandon the status quo. And as the leader, I had to make it happen with both decisiveness and sensitivity. To keep the same level of commitment they had shown to red wagons, I couldn't just dictate change, I had to orchestrate it. That involved applying several strategies – ones I've replicated many times in response to the never-ending need to move in new directions.

First, I complimented the elves on their history of red-wagon excellence and expressed my pride in their past accomplishments. *Next*, I introduced the change we were facing and explained *why* it was necessary. I laid out the facts – the raw data and evidence – and asked if anyone interpreted the information differently than I did. After some discussion, they acknowledged (some begrudgingly) that my read was correct. *Then*, we discussed the benefits to be gained – individually and collectively – for making the required change. Of course, the two biggest benefits were "staying in business" and "staying employed." Immediately *after that*, I asked for everyone's commitment to the new direction ... and got it. I reciprocated with two commitments of my own: 1) To provide the training and support that employees would need to make the changes – and feel good about themselves in the process, and 2) To demonstrate patience and understanding as they worked their way through the new learning curve. *Finally*, I made sure that everyone on the team understood that change of this nature was inevitable – we had no choice whether or not it would come. Our only choice was how we responded to it.

How have they responded? Just see what's out there next holiday season. You'll find a lot more than red wagons ... and an equal amount of smiling little faces!

REMEMBER: THE CUSTOMER IS REALLY IN CHARGE

There are many catalysts for the changes we're continually having to make. Some come from the development of new technology and equipment that allow us to do our jobs better and faster – like our board-game shrink wrapper and labeler. Others come from the analysis of ideas and strategies that didn't work – like our toy Edsel campaign. (We found thousands of them under trees, one year later, with notes saying: "You can have this back.") Several of our changes are spurred by monitoring the successes and failures of our competition. And still others are the result of hiring new employees who bring new ideas and experiences with them to the workshop. But unquestionably, the largest amount of the changes we face and make originate from the need to respond to our customers – as with the red wagon situation.

Like you, we are – first and foremost – in the customer service business. For us, no customers equals no business. If the people we serve were to stop writing, close their fireplace dampers, and disappear from the sleigh's radar screen, we would eventually vanish as well. Obviously, our job is to give people what they're looking for. And as their wants and needs change, we have to change along with them. Doing that starts with accepting the fact that the customer is truly in charge of our business, and then continues by setting into place plans for looking outside our snow-covered walls to make sure we have our fingers on the pulse of the market.

For us, the name of the game quickly became FIELD TRIPS ... a lot more field trips than the once-a-year pilgrimage experienced only by me, a harness full of reindeer, and the couple of elves who ride shotgun on the sleigh.

We do *virtual* field trips – through letters, e-mails, telephone calls, and internet research. And we do *actual* field trips where, on a rotational basis, we send employees South, incognito. Their purpose: To meet and greet, and find out what's happening with both *our* customers and our competitors ... and *their* customers.

We now follow up on all of the letters we receive – not just to make sure we have the orders right, but also to identify and track trends ... and to collect information on desired products, features, and accessories that we can build into our new toy development process. And we're constantly monitoring our competition to keep up with who's selling what ... and how the marketplace appears to be responding to it.

To be sure, the information we collect on our "field trips" is valuable and beneficial. But the *process* of collecting that data has proven to be even more beneficial. It's helped the elves and reindeer understand (better than any training program could convey) that everything we do revolves around customers ... and that changing to meet their needs is a good thing. Now employees are actually *recommending* change instead of being "victims" of it and lamenting that the old guy in the red suit can't seem to make up his mind.

TEACH "THE BUSINESS" OF THE BUSINESS

Our experiences both with red wagons and the whole field trip strategy led me to an important conclusion – which has since become a key Santa leadership principle: **The more employees understand about how the business works, the more likely they are to accept and support change.**

Having reviewed our employee database, I was keenly aware that we had very few business or finance majors on staff. In fact, many of our folks had never completed any type of basic business course at all. And those who did had pretty much forgotten what they had learned. Armed with that knowledge, I decided to take things to the next level by providing all the elves and reindeer with in-depth information and education about how our organization operates and what's involved in keeping it going.

I started by having our training group develop and conduct a basic business literacy course through which everyone would learn concepts like "cash flow," "cost of goods sold" (in our case, cost of goods *delivered*), and "first/last in, first out" (FIFO and LIFO).

I then "opened up the books" – giving the staff more access to financial information such as production costs, overhead expenses, and the like. And we gave that information true meaning by teaching the elves and reindeer how to read and interpret the data ... and how to *use* it in the performance of their jobs.

That was followed by instituting regular STATE OF THE WORK-SHOP meetings to keep everyone informed about what's happening (future plans, new products, planned purchases and upgrades, staffing issues, field trip reports, etc.).

A series of brainstorming exercises led to three other highly successful initiatives:

- Having different elves and reindeer attend, observe, and even participate in nonconfidential senior-staff meetings;

- Cross-training and rotating assignments within departments so employees can understand and appreciate the functions of, and challenges faced by, their coworkers;

- A departmental "swap" program that allows individuals to experience how other business units operate ... and how we're all interdependent in achieving our overall mission.

For us, teaching "the business" of the business has been *good business*. It's given the elves and reindeer additional opportunities to get involved in what we do, it's helped them grow and develop, and it's produced greater workshop-wide acceptance, support, and understanding of the need for change.

Most importantly, it's made them feel like true "partners" in the running of our North Pole operation ... because THEY ARE!

GET BEYOND THE RED WAGONS

- Help Everyone Accept The Reality Of Change

- Remember: The Customer Is Really In Charge

- Teach "The Business" Of The Business

6 Share The Milk and Cookies

HELP THEM SEE THE DIFFERENCE THEY MAKE

One of the biggest benefits of being Santa Claus is the fact that I'm on "the point." Although most everyone works his or her little ears and antlers off to make sure our mission is accomplished, *I'm* the one usually in the spotlight. Who are the zillions of letters we receive each year addressed to? Me. Who gets the credit for the elf-made presents found under all those trees each year? Me. Who enjoys milk and freshly baked cookies in warm homes while the reindeer try to catch their breaths on cold rooftops? Me again. And who is the only member of our North Pole team who regularly gets to get out and see, firsthand, the smiles that our work produces? Yep, you guessed it ... it's me.

Those benefits (and many more like them) are a large part of what gets and keeps me motivated. They're great – great, that is, if you happen to be *me*. But, unfortunately, there's only one Santa. And, with the exception of an occasional field trip, most of the elves and reindeer don't get to see and experience the same things that I do. So their feelings of satisfaction and accomplishment must come in different ways – from other sources. As the leader, I play a critical role in making that a reality.

A key strategy I apply in performing that role is to help each elf and reindeer see the positive differences that he or she is making for those we serve ... and for each other; I help them see *their* part of the big "making-people-happy" picture.

I start out by spending time with all members of the workshop team discussing how their functions, efforts, and contributions are vital to what we do. It's not unusual for me to pull a box of crayons out of my sack and draw a diagram – showing the physical link between an elf or reindeer (on one side) and a smiling child holding a present (on the other side). Doing that reinforces two messages that I'm constantly communicating to the staff: 1) We don't make and deliver toys, we make and deliver *happiness*, and 2) We couldn't do that without YOU!

I also make sure that everyone sees the scores of thank you letters that start coming in around mid-January. I post them on a large board in the workshop that's labeled: SEE WHAT YOU MADE HAPPEN. I also post my reply (thank you for the thank you) letters – which always begin with the words, "On behalf of all the elves and reindeer ...." And I often ask members of the staff to write and sign the replies themselves.

Finally, I take a few elves with me on each season's delivery run. When we return, I call a total-team meeting at which my traveling companions and I share our experiences with everyone.

Nothing motivates employees more than knowing they're making a difference. Find ways to make that happen in *your* workshop.

DO RIGHT BY THOSE WHO DO RIGHT

I admit it. There was a period, long ago, when I had fallen into the trap of taking my workers for granted. Things were running smoothly. The elves were cranking out quality toys by the thousands. And the reindeer were pulling the sleigh through the midnight sky at what is now called "warp speed." When an occasional problem arose, staff members dealt with it and fixed it. That was, after all, their job ... it was what they were expected to do. And as always, I was very busy. So I regularly responded with NO RESPONSE. I said and did nothing as long as my expectations were being met.

Then one afternoon, as we were loading the sleigh for our big run, one of the elves asked a very profound question. "Hey boss," he said, "good little girls and boys get all these toys. What do good elves and reindeer get?" Hmmm. I thought about those words all eve long. By the time we returned to the North Pole, I realized that I had failed to apply one of the basic premises of our business to my employees: Good performance should be reinforced with positive consequences.

I decided, then and there, to forget the typical *Elves shouldn't be rewarded for just doing their jobs* and *I'm too busy to give recognition* rationalizations. I chose to make a change – one that definitely turned out to be for the better ... for everyone.

Since that experience, I've worked hard at developing one of the most important characteristics of effective leadership: an "attitude of gratitude." I've learned to truly appreciate workers who meet or exceed my expectations. More importantly, I've learned to *show* that appreciation through my actions and behaviors. I look for, and seize, opportunities to give verbal and written atta-elves (and atta-deers) – opportunities to say *thank you* for doing right.

Now, when someone in the shop does consistently good work over an extended period, or exhibits things like exceptional attendance and conduct, I give him or her the recognition that is due. Whenever individuals or teams go "above and beyond" or make special contributions, I reward them. When staff members display behaviors that support important values like integrity, customer service, teamwork, and responsibility, I commend them. And there's no question that the elves and reindeer appreciate *my* appreciation.

I've learned that recognizing employees – doing right by those who do right – is one of the best things I can do for my elves and reindeer – and for myself as well. *I* feel good when I do it ... *they* feel good when they receive it ... and they're more motivated, and therefore more likely, to repeat the performance I want and need in the future.

Everyone wins. What a deal. It's happy holidays for all!

EXPAND THE REINFORCEMENT POSSIBILITIES

Now that I'm a (self-declared) "share the glory and pass the recognition" zealot, I operate by a simple rule of thumb: The more reinforcement of good work, the merrier. But that's not necessarily an easy rule to live by. Why? Because of two misconceptions common in workshops across the land: 1) "There's very little we can do. Money and options are limited." and 2) "Recognition and reinforcement are strictly management activities, and we only have so many managers." Those same beliefs existed here once upon a time – especially in *my* head. And I knew they needed to be overcome. The solution was as clear as an unshaken snow globe: We needed more *things* to do, and more *people* doing them.

We tackled the first misconception with thought and creativity. I worked on my own, and then with my team leaders, to develop a list of low-cost, high-impact ways to recognize our elves and reindeer. We challenged ourselves to come up with as many ideas as possible – ideas that went beyond the typical pat on the back and armed us with different North Pole strokes for different North Pole folks. I was absolutely amazed at how many items we came up with. From letters home to families, to special training and assignments – from prime spots in the employee sleigh lot, to appreciation certificates we printed in the shop – from nominations for our formal awards program, to springing for (you knew it was coming) milk and cookies – the possibilities were and are endless!

Addressing the second misconception – that reinforcing and recognizing good work was management's job alone – proved to be a horse (make that reindeer) of a different color ... and a bit more challenging. The task was to get workshop-wide acceptance of the notion that recognition was *everyone's* job ... everyone's responsibility. And that meant changing some long-held beliefs and accompanying behaviors.

I started with real workshop examples to help everyone see how we ALL benefit from the good work of individual elves, reindeer, and team leaders. Then I asked for a show of hands and hooves of those who regularly praised their coworkers. As expected, the count was very small. When I asked why that was, the most common response was, "That's your job, not ours." I responded with, "Why is that? Who made that rule? Why shouldn't everyone be grateful ... and show it?" No one had a good answer. The "why" questions definitely had made the point.

I immediately asked them all to give it a try, and they agreed. I made and distributed a sheet listing ways to recognize and reinforce coworker performance. And I've kept the concept alive by talking about it at staff meetings, doing it myself, and by making sure I give recognition to those who recognize others.

Look for ways to expand the reinforcement possibilities where you work. Make that previously mentioned "attitude of gratitude" one of *your* most important workshop values.

SHARE THE MILK AND COOKIES

- Help Them See The Difference They Make

- Do Right By Those Who Do Right

- Expand The Reinforcement Possibilities

7 Find Out Who's Naughty and Nice

CONFRONT PERFORMANCE PROBLEMS ... EARLY

I don't know about you, but for me, the one aspect of leadership that I find the most difficult and distasteful is dealing with employee performance problems. Don't really care for it. Never have, doubt that I ever will. It can suck the jolly right out of you and turn "Ho Ho's" into "Woe Woe's." But since occasional problems are inevitable, and since it *is* the leader's job to address them, this is an area that I've really worked on. And I've gotten better – much better at it – primarily through my experiences with one "Igor The Elf."

Igor was one of the original elves here at the Pole when we started this business. I was new to the job – anxious to make my mark on the world and expecting that each employee would perform well ... and that I would be liked by everyone, all the time. I wanted things nice. I liked nice. And when he started, Igor was just that – nice. But things slowly began to change. I noticed that Igor would occasionally start his shift a few minutes late and take longer than scheduled breaks and lunches. My response was NO response – which I rationalized with "I'll let it slide because he does good work," and "It's no real problem right now. But if it becomes one, you can bet I'll act." Both of those were code phrases for what I realized deep inside: "I don't have the courage to do what I know needs to be done." So, I overlooked Igor's tardiness (Mistake #1) – hoping that it would magically go away on its own. Of course, it didn't ... it continued. Then, instead of dealing with Igor one-on-one, I chose to send out a memo to the entire workshop staff reminding everyone of the importance of being on time (Mistake #2). I hoped Igor would read it, get the message, and correct the problem without my involvement. Of course, he didn't. And all the other elves were left wondering why I sent a reminder about something they already knew and were abiding by.

As the problem continued, I looked for every excuse to avoid a confrontation (Mistake #3). But the issue came to a head when one of the other elves approached me and asked, "When are you gonna do something about Igor? His being late all the time is really unfair to the rest of us." The elf was right. I knew I had to do something, and I was furious that Igor had put me in this position. So I called him into my office and unloaded on him (Mistake #4). We were both angry and the tension was high. And then *he* asked a question that shut me up faster than a raised eyebrow from Mrs. Claus: "If this issue is so important, why didn't you say something to me sooner?" There was no good answer to offer, only excuses – the same type of excuses I wouldn't accept from others. I *had* been unfair to the other elves ... and to Igor as well. I'd seen something I didn't like – something I knew was wrong – and I had failed to do anything about it. I was as much to blame for Igor's continuing problem as he was ... and I knew it. I swore, then and there, never to let that happen again. And I haven't. Now I deal with performance problems early and calmly – before they get big.

COACH "THE MAJORITY IN THE MIDDLE"

W hat do you think about when you gaze at the sky on a clear night? What do you see? For me – especially when I'm driving the sleigh through the heavens on our big delivery run – I see stars ... lots of them. And those stars remind me of my elves and reindeer. There are **falling stars** that represent the few employees who exhibit performance problems like Igor, and there are bright novas – the **super stars** that represent the opposite in employee performance – whom I'll discuss in the next section. Most of the lights in the sky, however, are neither falling stars nor super novas. They're what I call the **middle stars**, and they typify the vast majority of our North Pole employees.

The middle star group is the backbone of our workshop. They're the good, solid workers who, day in, day out, bring our mission to life. And many of them have either positive or negative potential; some have the capacity to experience super-stardom, while others run the risk of slipping into the falling-star ranks.

Obviously, for us to be successful, it's imperative that these middle stars avoid falling backwards. They need to stay as good performers or, better yet, move to the superior-performer level. And as a leader, I play *the* critical role in making that happen. I meet that responsibility by applying various strategies and techniques that fall within the broad management category known as "coaching."

Certainly, the term "coaching" means different things to different people. And one could argue that there are almost as many components *to it* as there are people who can benefit *from it*. But, since the older I get the more simple I like things, I've come to define coaching very simply: Helping the elves and reindeer avoid problems and do the best work that they can. And doing that with my middle stars includes the following:

- Making sure that they know and understand the performance expectations that come with employment;

- Providing the training and resources they need to meet those expectations;

- Giving frequent and specific feedback on how they're doing;

- Identifying any obstacles they may be facing, and then doing my best to eliminate those barriers;

- Teaching them how to set, manage, and achieve goals;

- Helping them learn from mistakes ... and successes;

- Hooking them up with mentors from the super-star ranks;

and, as I learned from the Igor experience ...

- Staying aware of what they're doing and "nipping in the bud" any problems that start to surface.

When it comes to managing the majority in the middle, the goal is clear: Make sure they avoid being naughty, help them stay nice, and work with them to get even "nicer."

DON'T FORGET "THE SUPER STARS"

Bet you didn't know that I'm a huge sports fan. It's true! I love sporting events of all kinds, and I watch them on television every chance I get (although the reception isn't always so good at the North Pole). I especially enjoy championship games and the Olympics because they involve "the best of the best" athletes – many of whom started in their sport with equipment from us.

Each time I watch, I note a very interesting fact: Before, during, and after their events, super stars spend time talking with – and listening to – their coaches. They ALL have coaches ... and they often credit current and past coaches for helping them become (and continue to be) the superior performers that they are. Why wouldn't they? After all, people don't *get* to the top of anything all by themselves. And few, if any, *stay* on top without help and guidance from others. That's the essence of coaching ... and the essence of this next leadership gift for you.

Your super stars earned their way into that category just like my top elves and reindeer did – by exhibiting consistently outstanding performance. And I used to think that the best thing I could do for those folks was to leave them alone and let them do *their* thing. Boy was I wrong! Like everyone else, great performers don't like to be ignored or taken for granted. Even though some may not admit it publicly, in private most realize that they need to be worked with, involved, recognized, and rewarded. In other words, they need to be coached. But with this group, the coaching role is a little different. For me, it's one of Santa the Encourager, Santa the Developer, and Santa the Cheerleader. And just like with the middle stars, I have several specific techniques I employ. I make a special effort to:

- Get them involved in decision making, strategy setting, procedure development, and problem solving;

- Delegate extensively and avoid "micromanaging" them;

- Encourage them to teach and mentor others ... including me;

- Celebrate their accomplishments and successes;

- Provide them with highly specialized training and other career-growth opportunities;

- Show interest in their work ... and their lives away from work;

- Hold their coworkers accountable for doing *their* jobs so that the super stars don't have to pick up the slack;

- Avoid punishing them for good performance ("You did such a good job handling that mess, the next time we get one, we'll give it to you again.")

As a leader, the key to dealing with super stars is to demonstrate – through words and actions – that you know and appreciate the fact that they are the *nicest* of "the nice."

FIND OUT WHO'S NAUGHTY AND NICE

- Confront Performance Problems ... Early

- Coach "The Majority In The Middle"

- Don't Forget "The Super Stars"

8 Be Good For Goodness Sake

SET THE EXAMPLE

If I've learned anything over the many years of wearing this red suit, it's that leadership is NOT for the paranoid at heart. Like most managers, I operate in a fish bowl. I'm constantly being watched. The elves are always looking my way to see what I'm doing. And the reindeer get cricks in their necks from checking on what Santa's up to at any given moment. They're all watching ... they're all learning. They're learning about what's acceptable behavior here at the top of the world – especially when it comes to matters of ethics and integrity.

Imagine what would happen if we had just one ethics slip at the North Pole ... just one time when we failed to do the right thing. It would be disastrous. Our excellent reputation – built over centuries of hard work and attention to detail – could be tarnished (or destroyed entirely) by a single inappropriate act.

How could the customers we serve ever believe in a Santa and crew who broke the rules, cut corners, or failed to meet their commitments? How could all the little ones out there be expected to be good, knowing that Santa Claus isn't? How could anyone even think of writing a "Dear Santa" letter ever again?

The answer is: They couldn't! And that would quickly spell the end of our legend ... and our business. That's why ethics is so important to us – that's why making sure that integrity "happens" is one of my most critical responsibilities.

You see, I'm the leader here. And obviously, I have a strong influence on the thoughts and behaviors of the elves and the reindeer. They rightfully assume that it's okay to do whatever *I* do. Regardless of what's said or written elsewhere in the workshop, my actions – whether good or bad – are the performance standards that they will follow.

There's no getting around it: I must model the behaviors that I expect from others. I must take the LEAD. I must be the first to "walk the talk" when it comes to things like:

- following ALL of our rules and procedures;
- treating EVERYONE with dignity and respect;
- ALWAYS telling the truth;
- NEVER breaking a promise or commitment;
- building superior quality into EVERYTHING I do;
- CONTINUALLY giving my best effort;
- CONSISTENTLY taking a stand for what's right.

Would you expect anything less from Santa Claus? Probably not. My workers expect nothing less of me either. And *your* people expect the same of YOU!

ESTABLISH GUIDELINES AND ACCOUNTABILITY

Because ethics is so important to us, I can't rely on my example alone for ensuring that everyone does the right thing. Certainly, I do my best to bring on workers who value and demonstrate integrity. And elves, in general, are a pretty ethical bunch to begin with. But they are human (bet you didn't know that), and therefore are susceptible to occasional slips, temptations, and lapses in judgment – as we all are. And, just like the rest of us, they need guidelines, direction, and clear expectations to help them stay on track.

So, I make sure that all staff members are well-versed in the laws, rules, and procedures that apply to them. We spend a lot of time discussing – in specific, "how to" terms – what it means to be ethical. And, to help guide their (and my) actions and decisions, we worked together to develop this:

THE WORKSHOP "WHAT'S RIGHT?" TEST

1. Is it legal?
2. Does it comply with our workshop rules and guidelines?
3. Is it in sync with our North Pole values?
4. Will I be comfortable, guilt-free, or even jolly if I do it?
5. Does it support our goals, commitments, and mission?
6. Would I do it to my family or friends?
7. Would I be perfectly okay with someone doing it to me?
8. Would the most ethical individual I know of do it?

All the guidelines we provide are valuable and important. But for them to have true meaning and really matter, they must be backed with accountabilities and consequences. Just as most children know that failing to be good can result in Santa skipping their house, everyone here at the workshop knows that doing wrong will likely result in a coaching session from Santa ... or worse.

For me, building accountability for proper behavior involves the following:

Keeping my eyes and ears open to what's happening.
Through visits, feedback, reports, meetings, etc., I make sure that I'm aware of *what* is being done and *how* it's being accomplished.

Providing ongoing feedback.
I regularly meet with the elves and reindeer to discuss their performance, share my observations, and reemphasize the importance of integrity-driven workshop practices.

Displaying "zero-tolerance."
Ethics violations don't occur very often at the Pole. But when they do, I take swift and deliberate action. I stop the offense, conduct an investigation, and initiate the appropriate consequences.

Think the elves might resent this level of accountability? Well, they don't. They actually support it. Some even demand it. They expect me to take a strong stand in preserving the principles that they take so much pride in having.

REMEMBER THAT EVERYTHING COUNTS

It was a Friday afternoon. I thought it would be nice to pay a surprise visit to a local mall and let children sit on the REAL Santa's lap for a change. After about twenty little ones came and went, Michael took his turn on my knee. "Well Michael," I asked, "have you been a good little boy?" "Yes I have," he replied. And then he continued, "I've been very good. Maybe I did tell a little lie. And I cheated on a game and called my sister stupid. But those things don't count ... do they Santa?"

How would you have answered Michael? Chances are it would be the same response I offered: "Actually, Michael, those things *do* count. Being good means being good all the time. There are no time-outs ... no crossing your fingers behind your back. *Everything* counts." That's the same thing I tell my elves and reindeer, and it's the same advice I offer to you as a leader.

When it comes to our business, we've never broken any laws (at least none that I know about) or fibbed about our finances. I'm guessing that your workshop can make the same claim. Most can. But, doing right involves a lot more than avoiding those big "corporate sins." I've learned that it's our day in, day out, seemingly insignificant actions and behaviors that determine our overall goodness. I constantly remind myself of that as I work to set the proper example and hold everyone accountable.

Here at the workshop, we *do* focus on the big integrity issues. But we also give equal, if not more, attention to the "small stuff." I challenge myself and my staff to periodically examine just how ethical we are by looking at ...

> ... the way we treat and talk about each other;
>
> ... the type of jokes we share;
>
> ... the little white lies we don't (or do) tell;
>
> ... the commitments we make and keep (or don't keep);
>
> ... the workshop supplies we don't (or do) take home;
>
> ... the "unimportant" rules we follow (or break);
>
> ... the level of quality we put into our toys;
>
> ... the fact that we don't (or do) use the sleigh for personal business;
>
> ... the way we respond (or don't respond) to the letters we receive;
>
> ... the credit we appropriately share (or don't share) with our fellow workers.

These, and scores of behaviors like them, reflect who we are here at the Pole and what we stand for. Looking at them helps us to understand and remember that being good and doing right are not *some*time things – they're *every* time things involving everything we do.

EVERYTHING COUNTS – for your people, and especially for *you* as their leader.

BE GOOD
FOR GOODNESS SAKE

- Set The Example

- Establish Guidelines And Accountability

- Remember That Everything Counts

Closing Thoughts

here's a question that has been pondered for centuries and probably will be debated for years to come:

Is Santa Claus a real person?

Well, *I* think I am. The elves and reindeer think so too. Mrs. Claus certainly believes I exist. And to be sure, somebody had to write this book. But truth be told, whether or not I'm "real" isn't all that important. There are, however, two facts that are *very* important ... and very real:

1. To survive and prosper, you and your organization must be able to achieve "big things" throughout each year;

2. You can't get those big things done without effective leadership.

Those are the reasons this book was written ... those are why you should pay attention to the information found in this special guide.

You see, **it's not easy being a leader**. Your job comes with many challenges and responsibilities, as you well know. But it is an important and necessary job. And it can be a rewarding one – if you do it right. Helping you do that is precisely what "The Leadership Secrets of Santa Claus" is all about.

With this book, you've been given a valuable gift wrapped in a bunch of good wishes. What you choose to do with it, however, is entirely up to you. As with other holiday presents, you can throw it "in the attic" – never to be seen again, or you can use, appreciate, and enjoy it ... and look for ways to pass the favor along to others. Hopefully you'll choose the latter.

There's no question that *your* elves and reindeer are depending on you – just as you depend on them. Don't let them down! Apply the concepts and strategies you've been exposed to within these pages. Take advantage of other resources and opportunities to hone your personal skills. Those are the greatest gifts *you* can give to your people, your organization, and yourself.

Most importantly, never forget that getting big things done all year long isn't about magic. It's about leadership.

Happy holidays.
Happy all days!

1 BUILD A WONDERFUL WORKSHOP

☐ Make The Mission The Main Thing

☐ Focus On Your People As Well As Your Purpose

☐ Let Values Be Your Guide

2 CHOOSE YOUR REINDEER WISELY

☐ Hire Tough So You Can Manage Easy

☐ Promote The Right Ones ... For The Right Reasons

☐ Go For The Diversity Advantage

3 MAKE A LIST AND CHECK IT TWICE

☐ Plan Your Work

☐ Work Your Plan

☐ Make The Most Of What You Have

4 LISTEN TO THE ELVES

☐ Open Your Ears To Participation

☐ Pay Attention To How You're Perceived

☐ Walk Awhile In THEIR Shoes

5 GET BEYOND THE RED WAGONS

- [ ] Help Everyone Accept The Reality Of Change
- [ ] Remember: The Customer Is Really In Charge
- [ ] Teach "The Business" Of The Business

6 SHARE THE MILK AND COOKIES

- [ ] Help Them See The Difference They Make
- [ ] Do Right By Those Who Do Right
- [ ] Expand The Reinforcement Possibilities

7 FIND OUT WHO'S NAUGHTY AND NICE

- [ ] Confront Performance Problems ... Early
- [ ] Coach "The Majority In The Middle"
- [ ] Don't Forget "The Super Stars"

8 BE GOOD FOR GOODNESS SAKE

- [ ] Set The Example
- [ ] Establish Guidelines And Accountability
- [ ] Remember That Everything Counts

Your Commitment Letter ... To Santa Claus

Dear Santa:

Thank you for sharing your "Leadership Secrets" with me. In response to this wonderful gift, I acknowledge my responsibility to be the best leader that I can possibly be. Toward that end, I commit to rereading this book often and to applying the following techniques and strategies – found within these pages:

_____

_____

_____

_____

_____

Rather than mailing this letter to you, Santa, I will leave it here – as a personal reminder of the promises I'm making to myself and to the people I lead.

Thanks for helping me get big things done ... all year long!

_____   _____
(Signature)   (Date)

Santa
Clauses

SANTA CLAUSES

WORDS TO REMEMBER

*People need me ... they depend on me. We're doing something
important here. And knowing that gives me the energy
to carry the sack, lead the pack, and keep coming back.*
Page 8

*Just how do I keep everyone, including myself, on track and
motivated throughout each long year – all for one long night's
big splash? The answer is basic and simple: through an
unwavering and uncompromising focus on OUR MISSION.*
Page 12

*You can't possibly focus on your mission without also
focusing on the folks that make your mission happen.*
Page 14

*... it seems to me that what makes a workshop wonderful
is not walls and ceilings, but what happens **inside** those walls
and **under** those ceilings ... it's not how a workshop stands,
but what it **stands for** that makes it special.*
Page 17

*Making sure that everyone knows what values are important,
and then helping everyone turn those good beliefs into everyday
behaviors is how leaders create a great place to work.*
Page 17

*The time I spend hiring the right way is nothing compared to the time I'll **have** to spend dealing with the wrong reindeer.*
Page 21

It didn't take long to discover that our "different" toy makers came bearing gifts. They brought new skills, perspectives, and ideas to the workshop. They gave us more than one way of thinking, planning, producing, and problem solving. They made us better, stronger, and much more in touch with the "different" shapes, sizes, and colors of customers that we serve.
Page 25

Our success – and resulting reputation for excellence – is the result of clearly defined goals combined with well-thought-out plans to accomplish those goals.
Page 28

Our goals are specific yet flexible – allowing for changing conditions and circumstances. And because staff "buy-in" and commitment are so important to achieving our objectives, I make sure that everyone has input in the goal-setting process.
Page 28

Once a reasonable plan is made, we immediately implement it ... We get things going fast, and then we make midcourse corrections as necessary. And the way we know how we're doing, as well as what adjustments we need to make, is through continual monitoring and measurement.
Page 30

... we'd quickly go out of business if we didn't make the absolute best use of our resources: time, money, materials, and the talents of our elves and reindeer.
Page 32

... involving workers in running the operation – and in making decisions that affect them – is a key strategy for leadership success.
Page 37

I pay attention to what my elves (and others) feel. Perceptions are realities for those that hold them ... and I must deal with those realities in order to lead effectively.
Page 39

I knew we had to abandon the status quo. And as the leader, I had to make it happen with both decisiveness and sensitivity.
Page 44

Obviously, our job is to give people what they're looking for. And as their wants and needs change, we have to change along with them. Doing that starts with accepting the fact that the customer is truly in charge of our business ...
Page 46

The more employees understand about how the business works, the more likely they are to accept and support change.
Page 48

Nothing motivates employees more than knowing they're making a difference.
Page 53

I've learned that recognizing employees – doing right by those who do right – is one of the best things I can do for my elves and reindeer ... and for myself as well.
Page 55

*... for us to be successful, it's imperative that [the] middle stars avoid falling backwards. They need to stay as good performers or, better yet, move to the superior-performer level. And as a leader, I play **the** critical role in making that happen.*
Page 62

Like everyone else, great performers don't like to be ignored or taken for granted. Even though some may not admit it publicly, in private most realize that they need to be worked with, involved, recognized, and rewarded. In other words, they need to be coached.
Page 64

Avoid punishing [super stars] for good performance ("You did such a good job handling that mess, the next time we get one, we'll give it to you again.").
Page 65

You see, I'm the leader here. And obviously, I have a strong influence on the thoughts and behaviors of the elves and reindeer. They rightfully assume that it's okay to do whatever I do. Regardless of what's said or written elsewhere in the workshop, my actions – whether good or bad – are the performance standards that they will follow.
Page 69

There's no getting around it: I must model the behaviors that I expect from others. I must take the LEAD. I must be the first to "walk the talk" ...
Page 69

I make sure that all staff members are well-versed in the laws, rules, and procedures that apply to them. We spend a lot of time discussing – in specific, "how to" terms – what it means to be ethical.
Page 70

All the guidelines we provide are valuable and important. But for them to have true meaning and really matter, they must be backed with accountabilities and consequences.
Page 71

*Being good means being good all the time. There are no time-outs ... no crossing your fingers behind your back. **Everything** counts.*
Page 72

To survive and prosper, you and your organization must be able to achieve "big things" throughout each year ... You can't get those big things done without effective leadership.
Page 76

Your job comes with many challenges and responsibilities, as you well know. But it is a necessary and important job. And it can be a rewarding one – if you do it right.
Page 76

... your elves and reindeer are depending on you – just as you depend on them. Don't let them down!
Page 77

*... never forget that getting big things done all year long isn't about magic. It's about **leadership**.*
Page 77

The
LEADERSHIP SECRETS
———— of ————
SANTA
CLAUS

The Leadership Secrets of Santa Claus ™
Softcover
Provide a copy of *The Leadership Secrets of Santa Claus™* to all your leaders today.

$14.95
(Quantity discounts available)

The Leadership Secrets of Santa Claus ™
Hardback Gift Edition
The perfect gift for every member of your leadership team!
$21.95
(Quantity discounts available)

The Leadership Secrets of Santa Claus ™
Audio CD
Narrated by Santa Claus
Perfect for leaders on the go!

$19.95

The 12 Days of Leadership
Building upon the 12 key strategies of *The Leadership Secrets of Santa Claus™*, this resource provides 36 practical, easy-to-follow tips for turning good intentions into actual leadership behaviors!
$2.95

The Leadership Secrets of Santa Claus ™
Workbook
The perfect companion to the book or audio CD! The workbook can be used as a self-study guide or as a component of a facilitator-led leadership development program.
$99.95 (set of 12)

Santa's Leadership Library

This collection of all of Santa's Selections, providing in-depth concepts and strategies, supports the material presented in *The Leadership Secrets of Santa Claus™*.

The library includes such popular titles as: *Ethics4Everyone*; *180 Ways to Walk the Recognition Talk*; *Listen UP, Leader!*; *Walk Awhile in MY Shoes*; and *WALK THE TALK...And Get The Results You Want* - as well as a copy of *The Leadership Secrets of Santa Claus™* Audio CD.

Santa's Leadership Library	**$179.95**

The
LEADERSHIP SECRETS
──── *of* ────

SANTA CLAUS™ ⓊTRAIN
Program

The Leadership Secrets of Santa Claus™ UTrain Program will enable leaders at all levels to become effective trainers. The program is designed to teach the basic principles of "Santa's secrets" and motivate your audience. This "do-it-yourself" resource includes:

✓ Learning exercises and discussion questions
✓ Easy to use PowerPoint visuals
✓ Group preparation suggestions and training tips

Once you order, you will receive instructions via e-mail on how to download the complete *The Leadership Secrets of Santa Claus™* UTrain Program. It's that easy! Please make sure you include your e-mail address on the order form when you order. Better yet, order online at **www.santassecrets.com** and download it immediately!

The Leadership Secrets of Santa Claus™ UTrain   **$79.95**

SANTA'S GOODIES

Santa's sack is filled with "goodies" to enhance your training activities. Stock up on these Santa-themed resources and use them as:

- ✓ Instructional props and training exercise components
- ✓ Rewards for training activity participation and achievement
- ✓ "Graduation gifts" for training program completion
- ✓ Post-training reminders and learning reinforcers

Be creative as you identify uses for these wonderful support products. They'll help make your activities special...and truly memorable!

The Leadership Secrets of Santa Claus™ MEM-CARDS™
Twenty-eight pocket-sized cards containing all the best ideas from *The Leadership Secrets of Santa Claus™* in a handy bifold wallet.

Pack of 12 MEM-CARDS™   **$89.95**

Santa Note Cards
As Santa says, "Share the milk and cookies!" Encourage leaders to send a compliment, an encouragement, or just a simple "Thank You" with these cards and accompanying envelopes.

Pack of 12 note cards   **$17.95**

Santa Pens
Reinforce the Santa theme and leadership messages by giving each participant one of these pens to use during training exercises and activities, and to keep as a fun and effective memory-jogger back on the job.

Pack of 12 pens   **$16.95**

Santa Coffee Mugs

Perfect for coffee, tea, or even milk (with cookies, of course!). And, they're excellent desktop containers for pencils and pens. Use them to add a special touch to your training events. They make wonderful gifts for everyone in your workshop!

Pack of 12 coffee mugs   **$99.95**

Santa Mouse Pads

Reinforce Santa's eight leadership "secrets" 365 days a year! These are perfect tools to remind everyone that "getting big things done all year long" isn't about magic...it's about LEADERSHIP!

Pack of 12 mouse pads   **$69.95**

Santa De-Stress Balls

Start your sessions with a fun icebreaker. Use them as exercise props or just reward participants with these squeezable Santas. They can be tossed or rolled. And each time they're squeezed, training will be remembered.

Pack of 12 de-stress balls   **$39.95**

'BELIEVE' Lapel Pins and Bookmarks

Use these to recognize participants during sessions - and as reminders of the overall message of the Santa book and video. Encourage attendees to wear them as a sign that they've completed training...and that they believe!

Pack of 12 pins and bookmarks   **$39.95**

Santa Hats

Reinforce the Santa theme by using these in learning exercises and skits. And consider placing one on the head of each participant at "graduation." These plush red hats make excellent bookshelf reminders of your training.

Pack of 12 Santa hats   **$99.95**

To order any of Santa's Goodies for your leadership team ...

 Please call
888.822.9255   *or*   Visit us online at
www.santassecrets.com

SANTA'S TRAINING
TOOL KIT

NEW FOR 2005!

This comprehensive collection of high-impact training resources and support products is designed to help you craft and conduct a high-impact leadership development program based on the concepts found in the best-selling book: *The Leadership Secrets of Santa Claus™*.

Whether you're looking to develop a brand new leadership development component or simply enhance your current training - whether your target audience size is five or five thousand - Santa's Tool Kit is a must for every training professional! This resource will help you create a memorable educational experience and get everyone in your organization energized and committed to personal and professional development. The tool kit includes:

- ✓ Comprehensive User's Guide
- ✓ The Leadership Secrets of Santa Claus Hardback book and Audio CD
- ✓ The Leadership Secrets of Santa Claus Workbook
- ✓ Santa's Leadership Library
- ✓ All eight "Santa's Goodies"
- ✓ Over 150 "Santa's Leadership Secrets" PowerPoint Training Visuals
- ✓ Santa's Leadership Secrets Training Video

SANTA SERVICES

Bring Santa's compelling message to your organization and help your colleagues get big things done in their "workshops"...all year long. We offer you:

- Keynote and Conference Presentations
- Leadership Development Workshops
- Train-The-Trainer/Certification Services

The Leadership Secrets of Santa Claus Keynote & Conference Presentation
A dynamic multimedia trip to the North Pole to learn how Santa and his highly motivated team of elves and reindeer accomplish their amazing goals. It's an entertaining and profound educational journey designed to inspire and challenge every member of your organization.

The Santa Claus Leadership Development Workshop
A highly interactive half-day Training Program designed to teach leaders, at all levels, Santa's eight practical strategies for leading others and getting big things done in the "workshop"...all year long.

Train-The-Trainer/Certification
A one-day "How To" Training Session with your designated "Leadership Secrets" Facilitator. This session will focus on customizing the program content to your organization's culture and giving your Trainer the skills, confidence, and resources necessary to effectively deliver Santa Claus' powerful message.

To learn more, or to schedule your
"Leadership Secrets of Santa Claus" event:

Call: **888.822.9255**

or

 E-mail: **santa@santassecrets.com**

☑ **Please send me extra copies of:** *The Leadership Secrets of Santa Claus*™

The Leadership Secrets of Santa Claus™ softcover ＿＿ copies X ＿＿＿ =$＿＿＿＿

   1-24 copies $14.95 each   25-99 copies $13.95 each   100-499 copies $12.95 each   500+ copies please call.

The Leadership Secrets of Santa Claus™ hardback	＿＿	copies	X $21.95	=$＿＿＿
The Leadership Secrets of Santa Claus™ audio CD	＿＿	copies	X $19.95	=$＿＿＿
The Leadership Secrets of Santa Claus™ workbook	＿＿	sets	X $99.95	=$＿＿＿
The Leadership Secrets of Santa Claus™ UTrain	＿＿	copies	X $79.95	=$＿＿＿
Santa's Leadership Library	＿＿	sets	X $179.95	=$＿＿＿
Santa's Training Tool Kit	＿＿	sets	X $895.00	=$＿＿＿
The 12 Days of Leadership	＿＿	copies	X $2.95	=$＿＿＿

Santa's Goodies (packs of 12)

MEM-CARDS™	＿＿	sets	X $89.95	=$＿＿＿
Note Cards	＿＿	sets	X $17.95	=$＿＿＿
Pens	＿＿	sets	X $16.95	=$＿＿＿
Coffee Mugs	＿＿	sets	X $99.95	=$＿＿＿
Mouse Pads	＿＿	sets	X $69.95	=$＿＿＿
De-Stress Balls	＿＿	sets	X $39.95	=$＿＿＿
Lapel Pins and Bookmarks	＿＿	sets	X $39.95	=$＿＿＿
Santa Hats	＿＿	sets	X $99.95	=$＿＿＿

Quantity discounts available. Please call for details.

(Sales & Use Tax Collected on TX & CA Customers Only)

Product Total	$＿＿＿
*Shipping & Handling	$＿＿＿
Subtotal	$＿＿＿
Sales Tax:	
Texas Sales Tax - 8.25%	$＿＿＿
CA Sales / Use Tax	$＿＿＿
Total (U.S. Dollars Only)	$＿＿＿

*Shipping and Handling Charges

No. of Items	1-4	5-9	10-24	25-49	50-99	100-199	200+
Total Shipping	$6.75	$10.95	$17.95	$26.95	$48.95	$84.95	$89.95 + $0.25/book

Call 972.243.8863 for quote if outside continental U.S. Orders are shipped ground delivery 5-7 days. Next and 2nd business day delivery available – call 888.822.9255.

Name＿＿＿＿＿＿＿＿＿＿＿＿＿＿＿ Title ＿＿＿＿＿＿＿＿＿＿＿＿

Organization＿＿＿＿＿＿＿＿＿＿＿＿＿＿＿＿＿＿＿＿＿＿＿＿

Shipping Address＿＿＿＿＿＿＿＿＿＿＿＿＿＿＿＿＿＿＿＿＿＿

City＿＿＿＿＿＿＿＿＿ (No PO Boxes) State＿＿＿＿＿ Zip ＿＿＿＿

Phone＿＿＿＿＿＿＿＿＿＿ Fax ＿＿＿＿＿＿＿＿＿＿＿＿

E-Mail＿＿＿＿＿＿＿＿＿＿＿＿＿＿＿＿＿＿＿＿＿＿＿＿＿＿

Charge Your Order: ☐ MasterCard ☐ Visa ☐ American Express

Credit Card Number＿＿＿＿＿＿＿＿＿＿＿＿ Exp. Date＿＿＿＿＿

☐ Check Enclosed (Payable to The WALK THE TALK Company)

☐ Please Invoice (**Orders over $250 ONLY**) P.O. Number (if required)＿＿＿＿

WALK THE TALK®	**PHONE** 1.888.822.9255 or 972.243.8863 M-F, 8:30-5:00 Cen.	**FAX** 972-243-0815 **ONLINE** www.santassecrets.com	**MAIL** WALK THE TALK Co. 2925 LBJ Fwy., #201 Dallas, TX 75234

Prices effective September 2005 are subject to change.

Four easy ways to order

The Leadership Secrets of Santa Claus
and
SANTA'S SELECTIONS

ONLINE
www.santassecrets.com
Visit our website 24 hours a day

FAX
972.243.0815

MAIL
The WALK THE TALK Company
2925 LBJ Freeway, Suite 201
Dallas, TX 75234

or
Speak directly with one of Santa's helpers
(Customer Satisfaction Representatives) by

PHONE
888.822.9255 (Toll Free), or 972.243.8863
Monday through Friday, 8:30 a.m. – 5 p.m., Central

The WALK THE TALK® Company
Helping organizations achieve success through Ethical
Leadership and Values-Based Business Practices